Kitanai and Lazy Lizard
GET FIT

by Thomas Kingsley Troupe

illustrated by Jamey Christoph

PICTURE WINDOW BOOKS
a capstone imprint

Kitanai the Origami Dog loved to run in the garden. Today he tried a new path through the green bushes.

4

5

6

7

Stretching helps make you more flexible. If you're more flexible, your muscles won't get hurt as easily.

That makes sense.

9

They ran in place. They did sit ups. They jumped up and down.

Now we're doing a warm up.

Here. Skip rope.

Yes, I can see it's a rope.

Hey! There's water coming out of my head!

That's sweat. That means you're warmed up! Sweat helps your body cool off when you're working hard.

13

Kitanai threw a football. Skip caught it and did a little dance.

Playing sports is a great way to stay fit.

19

GLOSSARY

barge—to move in with force

break—a pause from activity

exercise—activities to improve health and fitness

squat—to crouch down by bending your knees

stretch—to straighten the body or a body part

READ MORE

Bellisario, Gina. *Move Your Body!* Minneapolis: Lerner, 2014.

Labrecque, Ellen. *Stamina: Get Stronger and Play Longer.* Chicago: Heinemann Library, 2012.

Smith, Siân. *Getting Exercise.* Chicago: Heinemann Library, 2013.

INTERNET SITES

FactHound offers a safe, fun way to find Internet sites related to this book. All of the sites on FactHound have been researched by our staff.

Here's all you do:

Visit www.facthound.com

Type in this code: 9781479560837

Super-cool stuff!

Check out projects, games and lots more at
www.capstonekids.com

INDEX

Editor: Jeni Wittrock
Designer: Ashlee Suker
Art Director: Nathan Gassman
Production Specialist: Morgan Walters
The illustrations in this book were created digitally.

Picture Window Books are published by Capstone,
1710 Roe Crest Drive, North Mankato, Minnesota 56003
www.capstonepub.com

Library of Congress Cataloging-in-Publication
Troupe, Thomas Kingsley, author, and Jamey Christoph, illustrator.
Kitanai and Lazy Lizard Get Fit / by Thomas Kingsley Troupe.
pages cm.—(Nonfiction Picture Books. Kitanai's Healthy Habits)
Summary: "Kitanai the dog teaches Lazy Lizard how to
get fit"—Provided by publisher.
Audience: Age: 5-8.
Audience: Grade: K to Grade 3.
ISBN 978-1-4795-6119-3 (eBook PDF)
ISBN 978-1-4795-6083-7 (library binding)
ISBN 978-1-4795-6115-5 (paperback)
1. Exercise for children—Juvenile literature. I. Title.
GV443.T69 2014
613.7'1083—dc23   2014022919

Printed in the United States of America in North Mankato, Minnesota.
102014   008482CGS15

Other titles in this series:

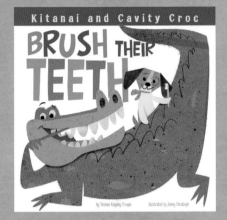